MW01004015

God's Will

Jakob Barrientos

ISBN: 978-1-64204-935-0

DEDICATION

Todd and Tasha Dial. Because of your
generous financial gift, I was able to see my
dream of becoming a published author come
true. I believe that many souls will make it to
Heaven because of your partnership.

I do not seek My own will but the
will of the Father who sent me.
John 5:30

CONTENTS

Acknowledgments   i

Don't Be Stupid   1

Test #1: God's Will   7

I Am Saved   13

I Am Spirit Filled   21

I Am Sanctified   31

I Am Submissive   37

I Am Willing to Suffer   45

So What Is God's Will?   51

Test #2: Heart and Hand   61

Test #3: Do Something   73

ACKNOWLEDGMENTS

In 2014 my spiritual father, Steve Hill, went home to be with The Lord. During his memorial service they played various clips and videos highlighting his life. An audio clip played at one point where he said he had done so much for The Lord he felt like he'd lived three lives. It was incredible to hear about all that he and his wife Jeri accomplished. Missions work. Church planting. Teen Challenge. Bible Colleges. Years of revival meetings. Crusade meetings around the globe. Spiritual sons and daughters. Books written. Television. So much more.

I learned how to discern the will of God by watching Steve Hill. His love for Jesus, his love for people, and his tireless work ethic have left an indelible mark on my life.

DON'T BE STUPID

Therefore do not be unwise, but understand what the will of the Lord is.
Ephesians 5:17

Everybody wants to know the will of God. I have met people in all walks of life that have a deep yearning to understand the will of God for their life. New believers quickly come to realize that they have the call of God on their life and begin to seek the Lord. Seasoned believers will go to conferences and prophetic meetings looking for a glimpse of God's desire for their life. Even individuals that haven't yielded their lives to Christ as savior tend to have a desire to find meaning and purpose in their life.

So why do so many struggle to know the will of God? Why do people of varying levels of maturity feel they are out of God's will?

Ephesians 5 says that if we don't understand the will of the Lord we are unwise. The Greek word that is used for unwise cuts a little deeper.

Unwise defined: Greek aphron - mindless, that is, stupid, ignorant, rash, or unbelieving.

So, one could rightly translate Ephesians 5 to say, "Therefore do not be stupid, but understand what the will of the Lord is."

Sounds harsh! The Bible wouldn't make such a strong statement if God's will were some great mystery. I believe that most complicate the will of God.

In my 15 years walking after God, I have had very few seasons where I felt I was out of God's will. Early in my faith walk I saw a few keys in scripture that helped me tremendously.

My wife, Leah, and I got married the day she graduated Bible college. Within 6 months we were pastoring our first church. At 25 we planted our first church (an extension of our first church). The Lord allowed us to travel in evangelistic ministry impacting many churches in the US and around the world. I have taught evangelism at Christ for the Nations Institute (CFNI). At 30 my wife and I planned our first arena crusade meeting that touched thousands in the Dallas metroplex. I have been on staff at one of the largest Assembly of God churches in North America. Today, as of the writing of this book, I pastor a church in Lahaina, Hawaii, and provide oversight to 10 church extensions across Maui under the apostolic covering of Dr. James Marocco.

I share all of this, with all humility, knowing that some reading this have accomplished much more for the Lord than I have. Yet I feel it's worth mentioning, because in the 12 years that my wife and I have labored in the ministry, I have seen many fall out of God's will or fail to step into His plan at all. There were individuals that were in the same classes, same church, with similar callings who have been "waiting on God" for a decade or more. I have come to realize that many people simply don't know how to find out the will of God. Even if they have received a great burden or prophetic word, they may struggle with timing and execution.

That's the reason I wrote this book!

There are three tests in the coming pages. The first test deals with a Biblical view of God's will. The second test deals with opportunity and understanding the timing of God's will. The third test will reveal if you are positioned for God's will.

Prayer: *Lord, I ask You to speak to my heart. Change my life. I want to know Your will for my life. I want to know that You are pleased with the life that I live. I want my life to make sense in the light of eternity. I ask You to help me understand Your word, Your will, and the leading of Your Spirit. In Jesus name, Amen!*

Discussion Questions:

1. Do you struggle to know the will of God for your life?

2. Do you feel you are in His will today?

3. What does it mean to "wait on God?"

TEST #1
GOD'S WILL ACCORDING
TO GOD'S WORD

Jesus said to them, "My food is to do the will of Him who sent me, and to finish his work."
John 4:34

This simple statement from Jesus came as His disciples were encouraging Him to eat. Jesus was in the middle of ministering to the woman at the well and the Samaritan crowd that was following her. Jesus was so set on fulfilling the assignment that His Father had given that He would even neglect some of the most basic human needs.

And we see that Jesus made similar statements continually through His ministry.

> *I can of Myself do nothing. As I hear, I judge; and My judgment is righteous, because I do not seek My own will but the will of the Father who sent Me.*
> John 5:30

> *For I have come down from heaven, not to do My own will, but the will of Him who sent Me.*
> John 6:38

How can we be mindful, as Jesus was, to the will of the Father? What if we don't hear the audible voice of the Lord? What if we don't have a clear prophetic word? What if there is no confirmation?

You may not have any of those things, but we do have the Bible. It gives us a clear picture of a few things that we can be certain of.

> *Every Scripture has been written by the Holy Spirit, the breath of God. It will empower you by its instruction and correction, giving you the strength to*

take the right direction and lead you deeper into the path of godliness. Then you will be God's servant, fully mature and perfectly prepared to fulfill any assignment God gives you.
2nd Timothy 3:16-17 (TPT)

Did you see how many references there were in that last verse to God's word giving us direction? If you struggle to know God's will, the Bible is the very first place we should go. God's word reveals a number of things that we can be sure are His will.

I want you to check yourself as you work through the next few pages. See if you are in God's will as expressed through scripture. If you find that you are not, don't worry! At least you will know what a practical step into His will is.

Discussion Questions:

1. Have you had a time where God expressed His will through the Bible?

2. What do you think Jesus did to stay in tune with the Father's will?

3. 2nd Timothy 3:16-17 says the Word of God can perfectly prepare you to fulfill any assignment God gives you. Do you have assignments that you have not stepped into?

GOD'S WILL:
I AM SAVED

*For this is good and acceptable in the sight of God our Saviour; **Who will** have all men to be saved, and to come unto the knowledge of the truth"*
1st Timothy 2:3-4 (KJV)

The first thing that God wills for your life is that you be saved. Is Jesus the Lord of your life? What is your level of commitment to Him?

I have seen people who begin to seek The Lord only when they are in a time of crisis or desperate for direction. When Jesus becomes our Lord, that means He controls everything about us. We do what He wants us to do. We go where He wants us to go. We say what He wants us to say. Our friends, our workplace, our worship habits, our hobbies, our alone time, should all reflect Jesus as Lord of our life.

Everyone wants a savior, but few are willing to submit to Jesus as Lord of their life.

Paul called himself a bondservant of the Lord (Romans 1:1), as did James and other apostles. A bondservant is the picture of someone who willingly sells themselves into slavery. It is a servant/master relationship. Even Jesus acknowledged that His will was not His own, but His Fathers (John 5:30; Matt 26:39).

If you want to be in God's will, you need to submit your will to Him!

Are you saved?

> *"If you confess with your mouth the Lord Jesus and believe in your heart that God has raised Him from the dead, you will be saved."*
> Romans 10:9

In order to be saved, there needs to be an outward action of professing Jesus as Lord (master, ruler) and faith in the accomplished work of Christ. If we do so, we will be saved. It's not difficult, but this is a decision that even Jesus said few make (Matthew 7:14).

Have you made Jesus the Lord of your life? Check your heart now. Paul encouraged a church in Corinth to examine themselves to see if they were still in the faith (2nd Corinthians 13:5). Peter encouraged something similar in 2nd Peter 1:10-11.

Are you confident that you are right with God? Are you sure that if you were to meet Jesus today you would be received into His Kingdom? This is the very first thing we must do if we want to be in God's will.

I want you to pray out loud:

Dear Jesus, I'm sorry. I have sinned and fallen short of your holy standard. I ask You to forgive me. I believe that You came to this earth, lived a sinless life, and were crucified. You did that for me. You died a death that I deserved. You took my sin on Yourself and offered me Your righteousness. I receive that gift now. I believe that You were raised from the dead. I believe You will return one day. If I'm alive when You return, I will be ready. If I meet You after death, I will be ready. Cleanse me in Your precious blood. Make me brand new. Be my Savior, my Lord, and my very best friend. Come live Your life through me. I give myself to You. In Jesus name. Amen!

If you prayed that prayer, and meant it, I believe you were born again. If you are not already, make sure that you get plugged into a local church. The Bible commands us to worship with other believers on a regular basis (Hebrews 10:25). If you are making this decision for the first time, or you are returning to the Lord after an extended season away from Him, I would encourage you to be baptized in water. This is an outward demonstration of your faith in Jesus. It's a way of letting the world know you have made a decision to follow God. Jesus said if we will freely and openly acknowledge Him before others, He will acknowledge us before the Heavenly Father on judgment day (Matthew 10:32).

Are you saved? If so you have made the first step in being in the center of God's will.

Discussion Questions:

1. Are you confident you are born again?

2. What does it mean to have Jesus as Savior? What does it mean to have Him as Lord of your life?

3. What is your testimony? When did you accept Jesus as your Lord and Savior?

GOD'S WILL: I AM SPIRIT FILLED

So then do not be foolish, but understand what the **will of the Lord** *is. And do not get drunk with wine, for that is dissipation but be filled with the Spirit.*
Ephesians 5:17-18

Now, I'm sure that some reading this are already saying, "Jakob, I'm reading this because I need to know if it's God's will for me to marry the girl that I like" or, "I'm trying to figure out if I'm supposed to sell my house" or, "How does this help me figure out if I'm going to move to Fiji?". I promise, if you will stick with me through these few points, by the end of it you will get guidance on what God's will is for every area of your life.

So, the second thing that we see in scripture is that God wills that we be Spirit filled. Simply put, this means that we are submitted to the Holy Spirit.

Without digging into too much theology, the Bible teaches that when we are born again, we receive the Spirit of God (1st Corinthians 3:16; John 3:5-8; Ephesians 1:13-14). Jesus also taught that those who believe in Him would receive the Spirit, and it would flow out of them like a river of living water (John 7:37-39). It says plainly in that passage that this would happen after Jesus ascended to Heaven.

On the day of Pentecost we saw the fulfillment of what Jesus promised. Those who were assembled in the upper room were filled with the Spirit and began to speak in unknown tongues under the influence of the Holy Spirit (Acts 2:1-4).

If you have been born of the Spirit (born again), you now have the capacity to be led by the Spirit.

Even if you don't yet pray in tongues, prophesy, or operate in the gifts. All who are born again have received the Spirit of God.

It is important, however, to seek after the baptism in the Holy Spirit. The primary function of this baptism is to give us the power to be a witness (Acts 1:8). With this baptism comes the ability to pray in the Spirit.

Praying in the Spirit has several benefits:
- It builds your faith – Jude 1:20
- It is a witness to unbelievers – 1st Corinthians 14:22; Acts 2:13-14
- It builds yourself up – 1st Corinthians 14:4
- It gives us direction to pray when we don't know what to pray – Romans 8:26

For the purposes of this book, possibly the most important reason to pray in the Spirit, is that we pray the mysteries of God. Literally we pray the perfect will of God. (1st Corinthians 14:2)

There are times that I'm stressed over a decision, but I spend a short time praying in the Spirit, and the answer becomes very clear. The will of God is revealed.

If you desire the baptism in the Holy Spirit, and the ability to pray in the Spirit, remember the words of Jesus:

> *"So I say to you, ask, and it will be given to you; seek, and you will find; knock, and it will be opened to you. For everyone who asks receives, and he who seeks finds, and to him who knocks it will be opened. If a son asks for bread from any father among you, will he give him a stone? Or if he asks for a fish, will he give him a serpent instead of a fish? Or if he asks for an egg will he offer him a scorpion? If you then, being evil, know how to give good gifts to your children, how much more will your Heavenly Father give the Holy Spirit to those who ask Him!"*
> Luke 11:9-13

Jesus said we just need to ask! He wants to fill us. Go back and read Acts 2. You will notice that when the Spirit was poured out on the 120 in the upper room, they all received! Nobody was left out. When Peter began to explain what was going on, he quoted the prophet Joel and said that in the last days God would pour out His Spirit on <u>all flesh</u>. Not just the guys who would go on to preach or minister full time. Men and women, young and old, rich and poor, all peoples, tribes, tongues and nations are qualified to be filled with the Spirit!

One thing that's important to note, it's not enough to be filled once. If you look at the original language in most of these verses, there is a sense that you are to be continually filled with the Spirit. Jesus likened it to a river that is continually flowing.

Being filled with the Spirit is not like a cup being filled. It's more like a ship's sail being filled with air to propel it forward.

Smith Wigglesworth said we need to be baptized in the Holy Spirit daily. When asked why, he simply replied, "We leak!"

Remember our first verse in this chapter? Paul said to be filled with the Spirit but he also presented a contrast. Do not get drunk with wine, for that is dissipation.

That word dissipation means empty, vain, or prodigal living. If you are going to be filled with the Spirit and led by the Spirit, you cannot live in a way that opens the door for other spirits to influence you.

The example of drunkenness is a clear one. There is a reason that we say people are "under the influence" when they are drunk. It's not a coincidence that we call hard liquor "spirits."

I share extensively on the topic of open doors and the influence of demonic spirits in my book _Dealing With Darkness_.

You cannot live like a prodigal and expect to be filled with the Spirit or led by the Spirit. This includes drunkenness, but goes beyond that as well. If you are having a hard time seeking the will of God, make sure that you have clean hands and a pure heart before Him. Blatant sin and compromise is a sure way to hinder the will of God for your life.

Prayer: *Lord, I ask you to fill me with your Holy Spirit. I want to be sensitive to your Spirit at all times. Pour out Your Spirit on me today and help me to live yielded to you in all that I say and do. Baptize me afresh. Use me in a way that brings you glory. Lead me by your Holy Spirit every day. In Jesus name, Amen.*

Discussion Questions:

1. What is the difference between being filled with the Spirit and baptized in the Spirit?

2. What are some things that can hinder you from being submitted to the Holy Spirit?

3. How important is the baptism in the Holy Spirit to your daily life?

4. Why does Paul single out drunkenness as a contrast to a Spirit-filled life?

GOD'S WILL: I AM SANCTIFIED

For this is **the will of God**, *your sanctification; that is, that you abstain from sexual immorality.*
1st Thessalonians 4:3

Sanctification simply means purification, or consecration.

When you are born again there is a legal declaration that is made over your life. You are declared "righteous" because of the accomplished work of Christ.

There is something that we call "the great

exchange" found in 2nd Corinthians 5:21. It is this: Jesus took our sin upon Himself, literally becoming sin for us. Jesus then gave us His righteousness, allowing us to become the righteousness of God. He took our sin and gave us His righteousness. Amazing!

This is the process of justification. Picture yourself standing before a judge where you are either going to be declared a sinner receiving the punishment of Hell, or righteous receiving the reward of Heaven. This will actually happen for every man woman, and child who has ever lived. For those who have received Jesus as Lord and Savior, the Father will look at us, see the righteousness of His son, Jesus, applied to our life, and He will declare us, "justified, righteous, and innocent."

After we are saved, or justified, there begins a process in each of our lives called sanctification. This is the process of God purifying us so that we become what He has already declared us to be: *righteous*.

This is a process, and one that we must

continually pursue. 1st Thessalonians 4:3 specifically mentions abstaining from sexual immorality as a part of God's will. The Greek word there is "porniea." This is a broad term that includes all form of sexual sin including fornication (sex outside of marriage), homosexuality, incest, pornography etc.

The same passage also includes idolatry, or literally anything that exalts itself above the place of God in our life. That can be blatant sin, but can include good things that take priority over God. This can be family, money, job, hobbies, sports, games, or even the function of ministry.

Solomon said that sexual sin and idolatry will literally destroy your soul (Proverbs 6:32). Paul said we must crucify the flesh (Galatians 2:20). We must present ourselves as a living sacrifice (Romans 12:1). We must discipline our body and make it our slave (1st Corinthians 9:27). We must be dead to self and alive to Christ (Romans 6:11). We must die daily (1st Corinthians 15:31).

The point: You must kill your flesh, or it will kill you.

God's Will

Isaiah 59:2 says that our iniquity (repeated sin) separates us from God so that He won't hear our prayer.

We must stay in the process of sanctification. Let the Holy Spirit purify you. When you feel conviction over an action or thought, repent quickly, ask God to forgive you, and turn away from the sin. Ask God if there is anything in your life that grieves Him.

This is the will of God! Be sanctified. Remember, this is a process. You won't be perfect overnight, and God doesn't expect us to be. Just make sure you stay in that process.

Prayer: *God I ask You to search me and know me. If there is anything in my life that grieves You, I pray You speak to me and show me the path to victory. I thank You for Your forgiveness. I pray that You help me be all that You've already declared me to be. I want to represent You well in all that I say and do. Sanctify me! In Jesus name, amen!*

Discussion Questions:

1. What does it mean to be justified? What does it mean to be sanctified?

2. What are some things that people may not consider to be "sin" but could become idols in our life?

3. Sanctification will highlight areas God desires to purify in your life. What is one area God is speaking to you that needs purified?

GOD'S WILL:
I AM SUBMISSIVE

*Therefore submit yourselves to every ordinance of man for the Lord's sake, whether to the king as supreme, or to governors, as to those who are sent by him for the punishment of evildoers and for the promise of those who do good. For this is **the will of God**, that by doing good you may put to silence the ignorance of foolish men.* 1st Peter 2:13-15

God wills that we be submissive. Even Jesus was submitted to His Father and He honored the authorities of His day, by paying taxes to Cesar, or the temple tax when needed.

Are you rightly submitted? Most reading this book are probably saved, Spirit filled, and in the process of sanctification. This is where some may start to fall off the bandwagon.

There are individuals that have left their husband or wife (not on grounds of adultery) for another relationship, and are confused why they feel out of God's will. This is a clear violation of God's word.

Possibly someone does the opposite of what their pastor or spiritual covering has encouraged them to do, and they find themselves outside the will of God.

Maybe you rebel against what your parents encourage you to do while you are still under their roof and authority, and wonder why you don't feel in God's will.

I could give many more examples. Peter encouraged us to submit to every form of authority for the Lord's sake. This includes your political leaders, your husband, parents, boss, church leadership and the list goes on.

I can already hear someone saying, "I'd submit to my boss/pastor/parents/husband…but"

The Bible gives us clear instruction on areas we are commanded to submit:

- God said we are to submit to spiritual leaders – Hebrews 13:17
- God said wives are to submit to husbands – Ephesians 5:22
- God said Children are to submit to parents – Ephesians 6:1-2
- God said we are to submit to governmental leaders – 1st Peter 2:13-15; Romans 13:1
- God said we are to submit to our employer – Colossians 3:22; Ephesians 6:5-8
- God said we are to submit to our elders – 1st Peter 5:5

Now, you are thinking, my boss/husband/parent isn't Godly… so I don't need to submit.

God's Will

Do you think that when God wrote these words He was speaking only about perfect parents, spouses, pastors, employers and political leaders? Of course not!

You submit to authorities as you do to God! You honor authorities as you honor God.

In every major transition in life I have always made sure that the individuals that were in authority over me blessed what I felt God was leading me to do.

Some people think it's crazy, but I would not have married my wife without my pastors blessing. When I moved to Illinois, I made sure that my spiritual father blessed it. If he said no, I would have honored him as the authority God had placed in my life. When I was offered a position in Hawaii, I told the inviting pastor that I needed to get the blessing of the pastor I was currently serving under before I made a commitment. If the pastor that I was serving under had told me, "No" or "That's not God" I would have submitted to the authority that God had placed me under and declined the invitation to Hawaii.

There is safety in submission. God uses the authorities in our life to protect us. There are many individuals in scripture that had to serve ungodly men, but in doing so they fulfilled God's will. Consider David serving a demonized King Saul. Consider Joseph being betrayed by his family, his employer, and ultimately serving the ungodly Pharaoh of Egypt. Consider Daniel, who submitted to the idol worshipping King Nebuchadnezzar. The list goes on and on.

The only time you see anyone blessed in disobeying instruction from an authority was in Acts chapter 4. Peter and John were imprisoned for preaching the gospel. They were asked to stop ministering. This request was in direct opposition to what Jesus had asked them to do. The request was opposed to what the Bible commanded over and over again. Their response was, "Whether it is right in the sight of God to listen to you more then to God, you judge. For we cannot but speak the things which we have seen and heard." (Acts 4:19-20)

God's Will

The only time you disobey an authority in your life is if they ask you to do something that is blatantly unscriptural.

Are you submitted? Are you submitted to God? Are you submitted to the leaders that He's placed in your life?

Submission is the will of God!

Prayer: *Jesus, I ask You to help me with submission. I acknowledge that all authority has been put in place by You. I choose to honor and submit because I honor and submit to You. Help, not only my actions, but my heart to be submitted to the authorities that You have put in my life. Thank You for the safety, covering and blessing there is when I'm rightly submitted. In Jesus name, amen!*

Discussion Questions:

1. Have you ever had to submit to a person of authority who was not a model Christian? How did you handle that situation?

2. Have you ever been protected, blessed or given an opportunity because of submission?

3. Have you ever had a person of authority ask you to do something that was unscriptural? How did you respond?

GOD'S WILL: I AM WILLING TO SUFFER

For it is better, if it is the **will of God**, *to suffer for doing good than for doing evil.*
1st Peter 3:17

These seem to get harder as they go along don't they?

Remember what Jesus prayed in the Garden of Gethsemane?

> *Not my will, but Yours, be done.*
> Luke 22:42

God's Will

This isn't a difficult one to understand, but it can be a difficult one to walk out for sure.

Some are seeking a change in their life and wanting God to move them because they are suffering where they are. Others may have already received clear direction from the Lord but they are still seeking because what God is asking may be difficult.

Just because you are in the will of God doesn't mean everything is going to be rainbows and butterflies. The Bible speaks extensively about suffering and difficulties that will come as a result of being a follower of Jesus (John 15:18; 2nd Timothy 3:12; James 1:12).

Paul was shown the things that he would suffer for Jesus in Acts 9:16. There was another occasion (Acts 20 and 21) where individuals tried to convince Paul it was against God's will to go to Rome, because he would suffer there. Paul knew he was in the middle of God's will, even though he would suffer for His names sake.

The question is, are you willing to fulfill God's will for your life even if it isn't easy? What if He asks you to do something that doesn't feel like a promotion? What if He asks you to lay down something you love or enjoy? What if God is asking you to do something, or go somewhere, that will separate you from friends or family?

I will say, in my experience, that God really does take us from glory to glory (2nd Corinthians 3:18). I don't want to paint a picture that if you follow the will of God for your life, it means you are going to be broke and miserable. Quite the opposite. There is nothing more fulfilling than being in the center of God's will. God wants to bless His people. God rewards those who seek Him (Hebrews 11:6).

Are you willing to suffer? This is God's will!

Prayer: *Lord, I'm so thankful that You were willing to suffer for me. You fulfilled the will of The Father God, because You were willing to suffer. I ask You to do a work in my life. I pray You bring me to the place where I'm willing to do anything even if it's unpleasant. I'm not asking for suffering or a hard road, but I make this commitment: I will go where You ask me to go, and do what You ask me to do, even if it's not easy. I pray this in Jesus name, Amen.*

Discussion Questions:

1. Have you ever suffered because of your faith?

2. Has anyone ever tried to convince you that you are out of God's will? Did that cause you to question God's will?

3. Have you ever taken an assignment that didn't look like a "promotion" but ended up being one?

SO WHAT IS GOD'S WILL?

Time for the results of our first test. Some of you have been diligent to work through the 5 questions about God's will. Now you're ready to know if you can finally marry that girl, take that job, move to China, or whatever the decision is you are seeking the will of God over.

How did you do on the 5 Biblical examples of God's will?

We see clearly that it's God's will:

I am Saved
I am Spirit Filled

God's Will

I am Sanctified
I am Submissive
I am Willing to Suffer

Can you say that you are those things? By this time hopefully you can.

Great! Do you know what the next step in God's will is?

Do whatever you want!

Yes. That's right! You can do what you want. Some of you are thinking, "What? That doesn't sound very spiritual."

Actually it's very spiritual!

Psalms 37:4 is a familiar passage. It says, *"Delight yourself in the Lord, and He will give you the desires of your heart."*

Do you know what that means? It doesn't mean, "Delight yourself in the Lord and He will give you what you want." What it means is, "delight yourself in the Lord, and He will give you <u>the</u>

<u>desires</u> of your heart."

Meaning, as we are seeking God and His will, He will literally begin to put His desires into our heart.

Do you know why I pursued a relationship with my wife in the first place? I wanted to! I desired her.

"You mean you didn't have a dream, or prophetic word, or some vision from heaven about her?"

Nope!

I was saved, filled with the Spirit, going after God, repenting when He spoke to me (sanctified), submitted to my pastor and leaders, and willing to do anything for Jesus. In the midst of that I met this fiery, beautiful girl from Hawaii. And I desired her! My desire didn't make me want to sin or compromise in any way. It didn't cause me to violate what I knew the Bible said was the will of God, so I pursued her.

God's Will

As we began to date, God gave us many confirmations (including dreams, visions and prophetic words) that we were to be together. He has blessed our marriage incredibly.

Now, since I mention confirmation, there are some who feel they need to have the will of God confirmed by 2-3 witnesses before they act on something. This is not Biblical.

There are a number of times that the Bible speaks about a word being confirmed by witnesses, but 100% of the time you see that in scripture it's not dealing with confirming a prophetic word or God's will. It's speaking about bringing an accusation against someone. Meaning, if you are going to take someone to court over a matter, or accuse them of something, you need to have some witnesses to back up the story.

The only reason I mention this is because I have seen individuals that have a clear word from the Lord, and even have the desire to fulfill His will, yet they delay because they don't have 2-3 confirming words. You don't need it!

There is wisdom in counselors (Proverbs 11:14; 15:22; 19:20), but if we have proper submission in our lives, you won't lack that.

Paul shared something else that shows how God leads us through our desires.

> *For God is working in you, giving you the desire and the power to do what pleases Him.*
> Philippians 2:13 (NLT)

God gives us desires! And the power to fulfill those desires.

I noticed this happening in my life almost immediately after being born again. I never had a desire to help the poor. God put that desire in me. I never had a desire to go worship with people. I didn't even like people. God changed my desires! I never wanted to go into ministry. God put that in me.

God speaks through desires.

I had the great privilege of being mentored by

the late revivalist, Steve Hill. The Lord used this man of God to spearhead the longest running American revival in history, the Brownsville Revival. I heard great stories of how God used this man, how close he was to Jesus, the miracles that transpired during the revival, and the millions that were impacted as a result.

The first time I sat down with this man of God, I had some silly expectations. I thought if I asked him a question he didn't know the answer to, he might just pray, go to the third heaven and come back with an answer. (I'm exaggerating... a little).

There were times I'd ask about the will of God for a situation. I was stunned by his simple response. He'd say, "What do you want to do?" or "What does common sense tell you to do?"

He did a teaching once about how many decisions the early church made because of "common sense" or because "it seemed right."

The early church didn't need the audible voice of the Lord, a "thus sayeth" or an angelic visitation to bless the work of God. They sought God, and His will as they knew it in scripture, and they did what they desired to do.

By this point, you are either praising the Lord, or feeling let down. I have two more tests concerning the will of God. They are much shorter than the first. They will help to further identify the will of God for your life.

Discussion Questions:

1. Can you identify any desires that God has placed in your heart?

2. Are there times you have not stepped out because of a lack of "confirmations" over an opportunity or desire?

3. Have you ever done something simply because it was a desire of your heart, or it just seemed right? Have you been blessed in that decision?

TEST #2
HEART AND HAND

Whatever your hand finds to do, do it will all your might
Ecclesiastes 9:10

Whatever you do, work at it will all your heart
Colossians 3:23

God speaks through desire! What happens when you have a desire for something, but you don't seem to have the opportunity to step into what you desire? How do you know God's will in that situation?

In 2017 God began to speak to my wife and I

about a major ministry transition. We came to
Oahu and Maui, where my wife had grown up,
for our 10 year wedding anniversary and
vacation. We had the opportunity to minister in
King's Cathedral and several of their extensions,
as we have on other occasions.

Something interesting happened while we were
on that trip. God began to give us a burden for
the island, King's Cathedral, and a heart to
connect with our family members that live in the
islands.

What was so strange to my wife and I, at the
time, neither of us had a desire to come to Maui.
In fact, we had been asked to come on staff, or
move to the islands on several occasions before,
but had always declined the opportunity. When
Leah had finished high school on Maui and
moved away for Bible college, she said she
would never move back. I was on staff at Trinity
Church in Cedar Hill. I had the great privilege of
leading one of the main weekend services under
the incredible leadership of Pastor Jim Hennesy.
I lead all the outreach and evangelism for the
church, which I loved deeply. I also had a

growing traveling evangelistic ministry that I was passionate about. My kids loved their school. We had just purchased our first home hardly a year before.

Point being, we were very blessed and satisfied where we were. When God began to open our heart to Maui it took us by surprise! How did we know that it was the right decision? Why would now be the right time when we felt like it wasn't right in years past?

While we were in this valley of decision, Leah and I sat on a beach in Kihei and walked through the first test that I laid out in this book.

We asked ourselves, "Are we in God's will according to His word? Are we saved? Are we Spirit filled? Are we sanctified? Are we submitted? Are we willing to suffer?"

We both agreed, "Yes!"

Then I began to consider the second test which hinges on the verses at the beginning of this chapter.

God's Will

These two verses say essentially the same thing. You will notice that there are two main parts when it comes to finding something to "do" for the Lord.

First there is your <u>hand</u>.

Do you have the <u>opportunity</u>? Can you put your hand to the plow?

Second is the <u>heart</u>.

Do you have a <u>desire</u> or passion?

There had been times over our first 10 years in ministry that Dr. Marocco had given us the opportunity to come into King's Cathedral and Chapels. The first church we pastored didn't have a denomination or fellowship they were a part of. Pastor Marocco offered to be that apostolic covering, as he was to dozens (now hundreds) of other churches. When we presented the idea to our church, the board in place wasn't fond of the idea.

I had the desire (heart), but the opportunity (hand) was shut down by the board and elders of the church. Not God's will.

Some time later I ministered in several of the extensions in King's Cathedral and Chapels. I was offered a pastoral position. As I discussed the opportunity with my wife, she didn't want to move back to the islands. Most of my family was in the area we pastored in Illinois and they were being impacted by the ministry. I didn't have a desire to leave. We had a passion for what we were active in at the time.

I had the opportunity (hand), but neither my wife or I had the desire (heart) to make that transition. Not God's will.

When we came to Maui to minister in 2017 God began to break our heart for the island. Leah and I both had prophetic dreams on that trip that seemed to affirm that desire. We were confused because of the shift in our hearts. Dr. Marocco was actually ministering overseas at the time, so we didn't have the opportunity to share with him what was growing in our heart over those few days on Maui. Nobody brought up any staffing opportunities to us while we were here.

We had the desire (heart), but was the opportunity (hand) there?

I ended up connecting with Dr. Marocco over the phone a few weeks later after he returned from his international trip and I shared about our desire. Come to find out, one of his extension pastors on Maui had come to him just a few days before sharing that God had given him the desire to start an extension in another state. This would leave the Lahaina extension in West Maui without a pastor. Dr. Marocco had already been praying about who would step in to pastor the church when I called!

This time the desire (heart), and the opportunity (hand) were lining up.

Before I made a commitment, I needed to make sure I wasn't violating anything in the first test. My main concern was about my current ministry and my current spiritual authority, Pastor Hennesy. If my pastor told me no, that the move wasn't God's will, I would have stayed where I was. I have seen people step out prematurely and end up hurting themselves, the ministry, or their families. I wanted to make sure I was rightly submitted to authority.

I was deeply encouraged when Pastor Hennesy blessed us. We quickly realized God had already been raising up the couple that could carry the ministries that Leah and I led. We put our house on the market and received 26 offers in less than 24 hours! We ended up selling our home for a significant profit in spite of only living there for a year and a half. We were sad to leave, but we stepped out with full assurance that we were in God's will.

If you are wondering what God's will is over a situation, ask yourself: Do I have the opportunity (hand) and do I have the desire (heart) for this?

You don't ever want to step into an assignment or ministry without a heart for it. That's dangerous ground that will end up hurting people. Just because you have an "open door" doesn't mean it's a God door. If you are called to something, God will give you the desire and heart for it.

On the other hand, you may have a heart for something but the opportunity isn't there, keep praying! Stay on the assignment you are on now. Stay active in serving Him in all that you do. When the time is right, the opportunity will be there.

One last note that I felt was important to share. When Leah and I were invited to pastor our first church in Illinois I didn't have confidence that it was the will of God. I went to Steve Hill because I had one concern that made me question if it was the right step for us.

We had the opportunity and desire to take that church. The problem was, I was scared! I was 21. Leah was pregnant with Moriah. We were asked to be the senior pastors of the church.

I remember telling Pastor Steve, "I think this is a God opportunity, but I just don't feel a peace about it."

He stared at me with his piercing blue eyes. "Peace? PEACE?" he shouted. "Do you think a soldier standing on the edge of a battlefield, knowing his commanding officer has told him to go into war, feels peace? No! If God has told you to go, you go!"

I think you get the point. Don't wait for a perfect peace to come into your spirit before you step into God's will.

Discussion Questions:

1. Have you ever had a door open that wasn't a God opportunity? How did you know?

2. Have you ever tried to step into something without either the heart (desire) or hand (opportunity)? How did that turn out?

3. Have you ever failed to step into an opportunity because you didn't feel peace? After hearing Steve Hill's words, how important do you feel peace is when deciding if something is God's will?

TEST #3
DO SOMETHING!

They were forbidden by the Holy Spirit to preach the word in Asia.
Acts 16:6

The first test deals with how we can be sure our desires are pure and how God will speak to us by giving us His desires. The second test deals with bringing our heart into alignment with our opportunities. But what about opportunities? What do you do when you never seem to have opportunities? What about when you try to step out and you feel like a door slams in your face?

73

God's Will

Act's 16 is a very interesting chapter. Paul is just beginning his second missionary journey. He's not new to the ministry or to God's leading. He returns to a church that he ministered in during his first missionary journey where he recruits (and circumcises) Timothy to travel with him.

The Bible doesn't indicate any clear instruction that is given to the Apostle Paul. No dove flies by. No pillar of fire. Paul doesn't trip and fall on a map. I believe Paul did what he desired to do. Possibly it was the common sense decision, as the largest people groups were in Asia. He journeys for several days toward Asia. Most scholars believe he was headed to Ephesus. Before he gets to his desired destination the Holy Spirit forbids him from ministering there.

Have you ever felt that? You go somewhere, do something, and you just feel in your spirit… this isn't right. I'm not talking about sin here, but there is conviction that you are moving the wrong direction. I believe this is what Paul felt in that moment.

So, they turn their backs on Asia and Ephesus

and begin to head to Bithynia, which is just north of were they started in the first place! Keep in mind, it's not a 20 minute drive. This is days on horse or donkey, pulling carts, walking for many miles. When they get to Bithynia, again the Holy Spirit forbids them from entering. There Paul has a dream about Macedonia (another weeks journey) and believes God is opening a door for them there.

My heart breaks for Timothy. Young boy gets recruited by a crazy apostle that circumcises you, puts you on a horse, and leads you all over the map for the first month with seemingly no idea where God wants him to go.

But look at the ministry of Paul the Apostle. God used him to extend the Kingdom of God in a more significant way than possibly anyone else in the New Testament. He wrote 2/3rds of the New Testament; mostly letters to churches that were planted as a result of his ministry.

Paul was not out of God's will for a moment. We can learn an important lesson from the apostle. If God hasn't given you clear direction

God's Will

DO SOMETHING. Anything! Begin to move. If its not the right direction, God will shut doors and redirect.

I get upset when people spend lengthy seasons, even years, "waiting on God" when they could be doing something. Lead a Bible study. Serve a church or ministry. Get in prayer meetings. Witness on the streets.

God will steer moving vessels!

Have you ever tried to turn the wheel of a car that is sitting stationary? It's difficult! Much more difficult than when it's moving. Even if you can muscle it, and turn the wheel, you will notice that your car can't turn until it begins to move.

I believe it works the same with with us. We can sit and contemplate, "Maybe this way is God's will" or "Maybe that way is God's will." That's like sitting in a stationary car turning the wheel. Until you begin to move forward, knock on some doors, make some calls, put in some applications, ask for a date, move some money, you can expect to go nowhere!

I encourage people to take a step of faith. Start to establish a plan. Begin to move forward. God will shut the door if it isn't right. He may speak to you in a dream, through a word, or through your desires, and redirect you.

I recently sat down with a couple to help them discern God's will for their life. They were not familiar with this book or teaching at all. They were trying to decide if they should move to Oahu, where his family is, to Phoenix, where her family is, or stay on Maui where they are currently.

I asked them first if they had clear direction. They had no idea, which is why they were so frustrated. They had pro's and con's for each option, but no leading from God. So I began to ask them the questions on the first test.

"Are you saved, Spirit-filled, sanctified, submitted, and willing to suffer?" We talked through each question and ultimately they were in good standing on all points.

God's Will

So I asked them both, "What do you WANT to do?"

They hesitated, looking for some trick in my question.

The husband asked, "What do we feel God wants?"

"You said you didn't know what God wanted you to do." I pressed.

"Yeah…"

"So what do you guys personally want to do? What is your desire?"

Both responded at the same time, "Oahu!"

My wife and I simultaneously said, "Then you guys are supposed to move to Oahu!"

We walked through the second test as well. They have both the desire and the opportunity to relocate. On to the third test. I encouraged them to begin to move forward. Plan the budget, figure out housing, school for kids, work situations, church, etc. They aren't planning on moving next week. They laid out a timeline that makes common sense. Now, if they begin to move forward and a door shuts, or God redirects, praise God! They have some clarity on the will of God. If God blesses their move and their opportunity meets their desire, awesome! They know they are in God's will.

This all may seem overly simplistic to you, but every major decision in my life has come through this process. From my marriage, to the churches we attended, to our first ministry assignment, when to have kids, three major moves, many financial decisions, and countless other decisions. The only time I have ever felt out of God's will was a very short season where I had direction from the Lord but didn't step out as quickly as I should have. I was still learning this whole process myself.

Today I look back on where we have served, and what God has done in and through me and Leah, and I can only praise Him. God has been faithful in His leading and direction. We have always done our best to stay sensitive to His Spirit, responsive to conviction, and quick in obedience. It's not always been easy or fun, but there is a peace in knowing that you are in the center of God's will.

Prayer: *Lord, I'm so thankful that You have a will for my life. I'm thankful it doesn't have to be a mystery to me. I pray that You speak clearly to me about Your assignments on my life. I will be faithful to serve You, obedient when You speak, responsive to Your correction, and active even when I don't hear from You clearly. If I begin to pursue something that isn't Your best for my life, redirect me quickly! Help me to live my life in a way that is pleasing to You and makes sense in the light of eternity. In Jesus name, amen!*

Discussion Questions:

1. Even if you don't have a clear picture of what the will of God is, it's important to do something! What are you doing to serve Him today?

2. How do you think Paul knew the Holy Spirit was forbidding him from ministering? Have you ever felt this way?

3. Having worked through all three tests presented in this book, do you now have a clearer picture of what God's will for your life is?

4. What steps do you need to make to get on track with His will?

MORE
TEACHING
AND
MATERIAL
AT

JakobBarrientos.org

There is a spiritual battle that is raging all around us. Most are unaware and unequipped to deal with spiritual forces of darkness. Dealing With Darkness follows the story of Jakob Barrientos and how he was introduced to spiritual warfare. This book will give you basic instructions of how to pray, walk in freedom, and to easily identify the activity of the enemy around us.

You can get Dealing with Darkness at JakobBarrientos.org, on Amazon in digital, audiobook and paperback, or on Apple Books.

Notes

Notes

ABOUT THE AUTHOR

Jakob has a burning passion to see the lost come to Jesus and to see those bruised and bound by the enemy healed and set free! After being arrested on drug charges, and God miraculously raising him up from a drug overdose, he's been on a mission to see God touch the lives of those who desperately need Jesus.

Over the last 10 years Jakob has led and planted churches, taught in Bible Colleges, traveled around the world for missions and evangelism and served on staff with several ministries and churches. Jakob and his wife Leah live in Lahaina, Hawaii with their two beautiful children Moriah and Gabriel

Made in United States
Orlando, FL
20 December 2021

12303539R00057